Farming & Recollections
Steam in Agriculture

Paul Stratford

First published in 2019

British Library Cataloguing in Publication Data

A catalogue record for this book is available from the British Library.

ISBN 978 1 85794 554 6

Silver Link Publishing Ltd
The Trundle
Ringstead Road
Great Addington
Kettering
Northants NN14 4BW

Tel/Fax: 01536 330588
email: sales@nostalgiacollection.com
Website: www.nostalgiacollection.com

Printed and bound in the Czech Republic

Title page: **Foreman** Built in 1980 to a Wallis & Steevens design, this is only a 3nhp tractor but still powerful enough to drive the Ransomes threshing machine

Contents

Introduction

The introduction of portable steam engines, initially to drive farm machinery, was followed by the introduction of the self-moving traction engine, which revolutionised the agricultural industry that for so many years had relied on manual labour and horses. The ease and speed at which tasks such as the cultivation of arable land, threshing, wood sawing and haulage could be performed virtually eliminated the use of horses overnight. Then came the introduction of internal-combustion-engined tractors; however, while this had an impact on the use of steam traction engines, the newcomers lacked the power and reliability of their predecessors.

The single-furrow horse plough was replaced by the steam ploughing tackle, which utilised an engine positioned at each end of the field, a multi-furrow plough being winched backwards and forwards across the field. John Fowler & Co (Leeds) Ltd became the largest producer of ploughing engines and tackle, exporting its products worldwide. Most ploughing tackle sets were owned and operated by contractors, as were most of the threshing sets, and the traction engine could not only drive the threshing tackle but move it freely from farm to farm.

Unlike the large ploughing engines, with their winching drum mounted beneath the boiler, many agricultural engines were equipped with a winch inboard of one of the rear wheels, which could be used for winching trees from woodland being cleared, hauling the timber to the yard and finally driving the sawbench.

Steam power did eventually have to submit to the petrol- and diesel-powered tractors produced by the likes of Ferguson and Ford, but thankfully many engines were saved from scrapping by preservationists who wished to conserve the part that the traction engine had played in the agricultural revolution.

Paul Stratford

Portable engines

Humphries Portable engines were manufactured from the late 19th century by the little-known Worcestershire firm of Edward Humphries & Co Ltd of Pershore; here one lies abandoned in a farmyard.

Above: **Ransomes, Sims & Jefferies** Portable No 14382, built in 1902, is one of the smallest portables manufactured and spent its working life on a farm in Chile.

Left: **Humphries** Portable engine No 219, dating back to 1850, has been restored and is still capable of driving farm machinery, although with the original wrought-iron boiler having been replaced.

Marshall 8nhp portable No 10193 was built in 1883 and exported to Australia. With the chimney folded down for transport purposes, it awaits being belted up to the sawbench.

Robey Portable engine No 25961 is driving an apple-pressing plant at Burley, cider having been an essential part of farm life in years gone by.

Right: **Ransomes, Sims & Jefferies** Portable engine No 43030 *Harvest Time* operates an appropriate Ransomes threshing machine and Ransomes straw baler.

Marshall Portable engine No 69778, built in 1916, powers a large Robinson horizontal frame saw.

Garrett 4CD tractor No 33981 is seen here driving a Marshall threshing drum.

Garrett Having completed the threshing job, No 33981 now moves to a new location towing with it the threshing drum.

Marshall traction engine, built in 1909, prepares to start the job of driving the Ransomes threshing drum with the arrival of a loaded trailer of sheaves hauled by the Nuffield tractor.

McLaren Traction engine No 1160 *The Favourite*, built in 1912, continues the task of driving the threshing machine as it did throughout its working life. Manual labour is still required to feed the threshing machine with sheaves.

Above: **Foden** A Foden threshing machine of 1903 vintage is powered by traction engine No 3384 *Wattie Pollock*, built in 1912 by the came Sandbach manufacturer.

Above Lefth: **Burrell** General-purpose engine No 2250 and a Marshall 54-inch threshing machine still require a number of farm hands to complete the task at hand.

Leftt: **Wallis & Steevens** 1903-built traction engine No 2680 *Liberty* drives a baler for the spent straw.

Marshall No 36258 *Punch* is paired with a Marshall threshing drum and a straw trusser, which sorts the straw into bundles suitable for thatching.

Left: **Sawyer Massey** Built in Canada in 1912, this is a general-purpose engine but equally at home driving threshing machinery.

Above: **Wallis & Steevens** Traction engine No 7102 *The Reeder Express* and a threshing machine were photographed at the Great Dorset Steam Fair.

Above: **Marshall** General-purpose engine No 37690 *Old Timer* drives a 1906 Marshall threshing machine and reed comber, used commercially to produce thatching straw.

Righte: **Fowler** No 8889, converted from a roller to a traction engine, settles into its new life driving a Ransomes threshing drum.

Burrell Single-cylinder traction engine No 3121 *Keeling* would have spent most of its life working on threshing contracts.

Allchin General-purpose engine No 1311 *Lena*, built in 1905, has travelled from Ireland to take part in a wood sawing demonstration at the Great Dorset Steam Fair.

Burrell Compound engine No 4014 *Pride of Devon*, used for threshing in its working life, is seen here belted up to a racksaw.

Wallis & Steevens 6nhp single-cylinder general-purpose engine No 8052 is seen in the Devon countryside driving a racksaw built in that county by A. Blake of Diptford.

Robey Single-cylinder general-purpose engine No 29333 *Wally*, built in 1910, drives an Alfred Pearce & Co automatic-feed racksaw.

Ransomes, Sims & Jefferies Compound traction engine No 42035 *Alicia Rose*, built in 1932, is at work on a sawbench at Much Marcle.

Lleft: **Fowler** Single-cylinder ploughing engines Nos 2872 of 1876 and 3195 of 1877 are seen in 1988, stored in a farmyard in Worcestershire awaiting restoration.

Above: **Fowler** The same two engines, now fully restored to working condition, are seen ploughing as a pair again at a Steam Plough Club event in Northamptonshire.

Left: **Fowler** Single-cylinder ploughing engine No 1368 *Margaret* is the third oldest surviving example of a John Fowler & Co (Leeds) Ltd. product.

Right: **Fowler** Single-cylinder ploughing engine No 1642, built in 1871, is another example of an early surviving ploughing engine built by Fowler.

Left: **Wilder** No 1281 was built by Wilder's of Wallingford using components from an 1869 Fowler ploughing engine, and is seen here hauling the plough across a stubble field prior to setting to work.

Right: **Fowler** 'AA7' Class ploughing engine No 15257, built in 1918, waits as the plough is drawn across the field by the second ploughing engine.

Left: **Fowler** BB1 No 15163 *Headland Beauty* and its four-furrow plough are ready to begin another steam ploughing demonstration.

Left inset: **Fowler** BB ploughing engine No 14712 *Wilbur* winches a cultivator to the top of the field.

Above: **Fowler** Z7 ploughing engine No 15673 of 1922, the largest of the ploughing engines produced by Fowler, spent its working life on the Sena Sugar Estates in Mozambique.

Right: **Howard** No 110, the sole surviving ploughing engine built by J. & F. Howard in 1870, is unusual in having the winding drum mounted horizontally across the rear of the tender.

Top right: **Fowler** BB1 No 15142 displays a working patina in a farmyard in Worcestershire.

HO 5832

Left: **McLaren** No 1541 is one of only two surviving ploughing engines built by J. & H. McLaren in Leeds in 1918.

Right: **Fowler** No 16646 is a smaller, less powerful Class 'K7' ploughing engine.

Above: **Fowler** TE2 ploughing engine No 15677 was exported to South Africa for ploughing but was found to be inadequate and relegated to light dredging duties. It is preserved in a museum in the town of Worcester, South Africa.

Above leftt: **Burrell** No 777 is one of a sole surviving pair of ploughing engines built by Burrell in 1879.

Left: **Clayton & Shuttleworth** No 44103, built in 1911, is carrying out direct ploughing, a procedure that was rarely used in the UK due to the weight of the traction engine causing compaction of the soil.

Above: **Garrett** No 33180 *Suffolk Punch* is a lightweight direct ploughing tractor, produced in vain attempt to compete with the advance of the internal-combustion-engined farm tractor.

Right: **Avery** American-design direct ploughing engine No 4332, built in 1914, is to British eyes an unusual design, having the cylinders mounted on a chassis beneath the locomotive-type boiler. The wide rear wheels helped to reduce soil compaction on the arable prairie estates.

Left: **Foden** No 13630, a much-modified 'Sun' tractor, demonstrates direct ploughing at the Onslow Park rally in Shropshire.

Right: **Fowler** No 4223 *Aethelflaed*, another Fowler single-cylinder engine from 1884 and once owned by Warwickshire ploughing contractors Bomford & Evershed, makes its way to the ploughing field.

Inset right: **Bomford & Evershed** were well-known rolling and ploughing contractors, ploughing engine engineers and manufacturers of living vans in Salford Priors, Warwickshire.

Bomford & Evershed converted a number of Fowler steam ploughing engines to diesel power by installing a General Motors Sherman Tank power unit in the tender and also modifying the winching arrangement for dredging purposes in the ownership of Bomford & Carr in Binton, Warwickshire.

Fowler BB1 ploughing engine No 15223 awaits purchase for restoration in the former Bomford & Carr yard at the closed Stratford-upon-Avon & Midland Junction Railway station at Binton.

Left: **McLaren** converted a number of steam ploughing engines to diesel power using boiler-mounted Mercedes power units, one of which could be found in the former ownership of Bomford & Carr.

Fowler BB1 ploughing engine No 15199 was converted to diesel power by McLaren in the 1940s, extending its working life with contractors Beeby Brothers for mole draining.

Fowler AA7 No 15365 *Sandringham* dredges a lake near Ledbury in truly difficult conditions.

Above: **Fowler** BB1 No 15333 carries out the dredging of a silted-up lake in Herefordshire; another ploughing engine is employed in winching the scoop across the bed of the lake in the opposite direction in a similar operation to ploughing.

Fowler Nos 14367 and 14368 are two of the six Z7 ploughing engines repatriated to the UK from the Sena Sugar Estates in Mozambique together with restored example No 15670.

Fowler Ploughing engines BB No 14712 and BB1 No 15222 work as part of a steam ploughing demonstration at the Great Dorset Steam Fair.

Fowler ploughing engine No 2479, built in 1874 and part of the Beeby Brothers contracting fleet, draws the plough the last few feet.
Mike Beeby, a decedent of the founders, is riding on the plough.

Above: **Fowler** BB1 No 15334 *Lady Jayne* and cultivator create a timeless scene from a bygone agricultural era.

Right: **Start of the day** One engine is already in position on the headland while the second steams across the field ready for the day's work ahead.